D0555723

END TIMES

OTHER BOOKS:

The Soon To Be Revealed Antichrist
Snatched Away!
Family Relationships
What The World Is Coming To

ABOUT THE AUTHOR

CHUCK SMITH, well-known Bible scholar and prophecy teacher, has lectured on the "end times" throughout the United States and Europe. He has visited Israel, the Land of Prophecy, on numerous occasions and has narrated several documentary films, including the TV special, *Future Survival*.

CHUCK SMITH

END TIMES

A REPORT ON
...FUTURE SURVIVAL!...

Maranatha House Publishers
Costa Mesa, California 92626 U.S.A.

Scriptural quotations based on the King James Version of the Bible unless otherwise specified. Translational emendations, amplifications, and paraphrases are by the author.

Library of Congress Cataloging in Publication Data
Smith, Chuck
    End times.
    1. End of the world.   2. Twentieth century—
Forecasts.   3. Bible—Prophecies.   I. Title.
BT876.S57   220.1′5   78-6468
ISBN 0-89337-011-8

PRINTED IN THE UNITED STATES OF AMERICA

Contents

Introduction

We are living in extremely exciting days. It's as if we were backstage at a play just before the curtain rises for the final act. The director is positioning all the players and seeing that the props are in order before he signals for the curtain to rise. So God has positioned the nations, and the world is ready for the last act.

God is winding up the final events prior to the return of Jesus Christ. It's just like standing dominoes on end in a long row. When you tip the first domino the whole line goes down in sequence. God is likewise aligning the world situations. He is getting ready to tip the first event which will trigger the series of events ultimately climaxing in the glorious Second Coming of Jesus Christ in power and in glory.

Before we begin to look at the situations, let me emphasize one point. I have no intention of telling you the day that the Lord is coming for His Church. I don't know that day. Nobody knows that day or hour.[1] But the Bible does say, "Of the times and the seasons, brethren, you have no need that I write unto you. For you know perfectly that the day of the Lord so cometh as a thief in the night . . . but you, brethren, are not in darkness, that the day should overtake you as a thief."[2]

God wants and expects you to be thoroughly aware of the times in which you live. He spoke of them in detail so you could realize, as these certain events take place, that the coming of the Lord is at hand.

Chapter 1

End Times, Part 1

Look into the Future

Daniel is one of the most fascinating books of prophecy in the Bible. Daniel, a young Hebrew, was captured by King Nebuchadnezzar in the first wave of conquest by the Babylonians against Israel.

One night King Nebuchadnezzar had a dream that greatly troubled him.[3] He awoke in the morning terrified by the dream but unable to remember it. The king was left only with the lingering and horrifying aftereffects.

Knowing that his dream had a message of strong significance, Nebuchadnezzar called together all the wise men, astrologers, and soothsayers in the Babylonian kingdom and ordered them to explain the dream's meaning. Their reply was, "Tell us what you dreamed and we'll tell you what it meant."

Nebuchadnezzar answered, "I can't remember. And if you don't tell me, I'll have your heads!"

They responded, "Never in history has a king made such an unreasonable demand upon his wise men."

The king retorted, "That makes no difference to me. Either tell me or you'll lose your heads!"

Then Arioch, the captain of the king's guard, told young Daniel about the king's decree. Even though Daniel was being groomed as a counselor, he too was to be executed. Daniel told Arioch to tell the king that there is a God in heaven who knows all things, and that Daniel, who served that God, was able to reveal to the king his dream and what it meant. Arioch told Nebuchadnezzar of the young Hebrew captive who served a God that could tell the king what he dreamed and what it meant.

Meanwhile, Daniel went to his friends and said, "We've got to pray.

Our heads are on the line. I told the king that I can tell him what he dreamed and what it meant. Let's pray that God might reveal it to us."

God was faithful and revealed unto Daniel the king's dream and its interpretation. In haste Daniel was brought before Nebuchadnezzar. The king said, "I hear that you can interpret dreams and tell their meanings."

Daniel said, "No, I can't. But there is a God in heaven who knows all things. He knows what you dreamed and what it means, and He has revealed it to me."

Daniel continued, "The other night, O King Nebuchadnezzar, as you were lying on your bed, you were thinking of the power and greatness of your Babylonian kingdom. Then the thought came into your mind, 'What shall come to pass in the future? What will happen to my kingdom? How will the world end?' So God gave you a dream and has revealed to you what will take place in the future.

"In your dream you saw a great image. He had a head of gold, breast and arms of silver, stomach and thighs of brass, legs of iron, and feet of iron and clay with ten toes. Then came a stone not cut with hands that hit the great image in its feet. The whole image crumbled and the stone grew up into a mountain that filled the whole earth."

Nebuchadnezzar shouted, "That's it! I remember now! It was terrifying! But what does it mean?"

Daniel explained, "You, O king, are the head of gold. God has given you a great and powerful kingdom which has extended throughout the earth. But your kingdom is going to be replaced by an inferior kingdom, the breast and arms of silver, which represent the Medo-Persian empire. That kingdom will be replaced by a still lesser kingdom, the Grecian empire, which was represented by the stomach and thighs of brass. That kingdom will be replaced by the Roman Empire, the legs of iron.

"The final world-ruling empire will be a confederacy of ten nations related to the Roman Empire, the feet and ten toes of iron and clay. During the time of this final kingdom, Jesus Christ will come again in glory and establish God's everlasting. kingdom upon the earth."

When Nebuchadnezzar heard Daniel's interpretation of his dream, he acknowledged that indeed there was no god in all the world like the God of Daniel.

However, Nebuchadnezzar later defied the declarations of God and erected in the Plain of Dura a great image of gold which stood 90 feet high.[4] By making it all gold, Nebuchadnezzar was declaring that no one would conquer his kingdom and that Babylon would stand forever. The king ordered all the people to bow down and worship this golden image and affirm that Babylon would exist forever.

Then God allowed Nebuchadnezzar to go insane. The king began to live and eat with the wild oxen in the fields. His hair grew long and covered his body like feathers, and his nails became like claws. He went totally mad until seven times or seasons passed over him.

It is unclear whether "seven seasons" refers to seven years or seven literal seasons. Nebuchadnezzar could have been mad for one and three-fourths years or for seven whole years. Regardless of how long, he remained in this condition long enough to know that the God in heaven lifts up and establishes on thrones and pulls down those whom He chooses. Then the king acknowledged the power of God.[5]

During the first year of King Belshazzar's reign, approximately 70 years after Nebuchadnezzar's dream, Daniel had a vision.[6] He saw a lion with the wings of an eagle. It was devoured by a bear with three ribs in its mouth. The bear was followed by a leopard. This, in turn, was followed by an animal that he couldn't really describe. It was fierce and terribly awesome and had ten horns. One horn rose up and destroyed three others. This horn then became a great power speaking blasphemous things.

Daniel's vision was much the same as Nebuchadnezzar's dream. The four animals in Daniel's vision represented the same world-governing empires as the metals of the image in Nebuchadnezzar's dream.

It is very interesting to see that the prophecies of Daniel have been fulfilled. The Babylonian Empire was overthrown by the Medo-Persian empire, the Medo-Persian by the Grecian, and the Grecian by the Roman. There has not been a world-governing empire since the Roman Empire.

However, according to these prophecies, one more world-governing empire is yet to come. Unlike the others, this empire will not be a single nation but a confederacy of ten nations.

In Nebuchadnezzar's dream the iron legs represented the Roman Empire; the ten toes were a mixture of iron and clay. In Daniel's vision, ten horns came out of the indescribable beast representing Rome. Both of Daniel's prophecies indicate that the ten-nation kingdom, the final world power established before Jesus returns, will be related to the Roman Empire.

The Common Market

As we look at the world scene today, we see the formation of the European Community, originally known as the Common Market. This is an organization of nations who have established treaties among themselves for economic purposes. These nations admit that their economic treaties are only preparatory for future political alliances and, ultimately, for military alliances.

Nine nations already comprise the European Community (EC). Greece has made application and has been unofficially accepted as the tenth nation. The EC is now working out the details of ratifying the treaty.

Greece was originally expected to be brought into the confederacy by 1982, but EC leaders now predict that Greece will become a full-fledged member by 1980. This will make the EC a confederacy of ten nations—the prophetic ten toes or ten horns, whichever you prefer. This confederacy is related to the Roman Empire because each nation in the EC was once a part of the old Roman Empire. Eventually, this federation will become the final world-governing empire.

There is always the possibility that Greece will pull away from joining. Spain, also formerly in the Roman Empire, could possibly become the tenth nation. Whichever way it works out, there will ultimately be ten nations joined in this end times federation.

You may say, "Chuck, we have to be realistic about this. Western Europe can never rise to world prominence as long as Russia remains a major threat to the European continent. Russia has been building tremendous military strength poised against the West in Eastern Europe. As long as Russia has such tremendous missile and military capabilities, she is too much of a dominant threat overshadowing Western Europe. How could the EC ever become a world-military, world-dominating power?"

I have to agree with you—you're absolutely right. Even though the nations of the European Community have a greater gross national product than the United States and could conceivably become the greatest *economic* power in the world, they can never rise to world governing stature as long as Russia is overshadowing them.

However, God has an interesting plan to take care of Russia. We will cover the details of the prophecy concerning Russia's overthrow and defeat in Chapter 2.

The Antichrist

Once God destroys Russia's military power, the final world empire will be able to take control. From this confederacy of ten European nations there shall arise the "horn"—a man of authority and power who will become the singular leader of this empire.[7] He is known in the Scriptures by various names such as "the beast" and "the man of sin," but he is commonly referred to as the Antichrist. He will oppose all that is in heaven and will seek to exalt himself above God.

The Antichrist will first come on the scene with a tremendous peace program and an entirely new economic system. He will work wonders and will be known as a miracle worker. People will stand in awe of him.

There will be an assassination attempt on his life in which he is apparently killed—but, miraculously, he will survive. As a result of the attempted assassination, the Antichrist will lose the sight of his right eye and the use of one arm.[8]

When the angel of the Lord revealed to Daniel the exact day that the true Messiah would come, he also included an interesting prophecy concerning this man of world power, the Antichrist.

While Daniel was in prayer near the time of the evening oblation, the angel Gabriel appeared to him. He told Daniel, "I am now come forth to give thee skill and understanding. At the beginning of thy supplications the commandment came forth, and I am come to show thee; for thou are greatly beloved: therefore understand the matter and consider the vision. Seventy weeks are determined upon thy people and upon thy holy city [Jerusalem], to finish the transgression, and to make an end of sins, and to make reconciliation for iniquity, and to bring in everlasting righteousness, and to seal up [to complete] the vision and prophecy, and to anoint the most Holy."[9] The word "week" (which literally translates from the Hebrew as "seven") refers to a week of years, or seven years.

Several events are spoken of here.

"To finish the transgression . . . to make an end of sins . . . to make reconciliation for iniquity" all belong in one category: they have been fulfilled. "To bring in everlasting righteousness . . . to complete the visions and prophecy . . . to anoint the most Holy" belong in another category: they have not yet been fulfilled.

Gabriel continues, "There are seventy weeks [sevens] that are determined upon the nation Israel . . . Know therefore and understand, that from the going forth of the commandment to restore and to build Jerusalem unto [the coming of] the Messiah the Prince shall be seven weeks, and threescore and two weeks [seven sevens and sixty-two sevens]: The street shall be built again, and the wall, even in troublous times. And after threescore and two weeks [sixty-two sevens] shall Messiah be cut off, but not for himself [without receiving the kingdom]."[10]

This is an amazing prophecy. For centuries the Jews had been waiting for their Messiah, and here God told Daniel the very day the Messiah was to come.

According to the prophecy, Christ was to come 483 years after the commandment to restore and rebuild Jerusalem. On March 14, 445 B.C., King Artaxerxes gave the command to Nehemiah to restore and rebuild Jerusalem. Exactly 483 years later, April 6, 32 A.D., Jesus Christ made His triumphant entry into Jerusalem.[11]

Gabriel said the Messiah was to be cut off without receiving His kingdom but, in being cut off, He would make an end of sin and make reconciliation for our iniquities. Just as prophesied, Jesus was "cut off" or crucified. It was by the blood He shed on the cross that He made an end to our sins and reconciled us unto God.

That takes care of the 69 sevens, but the angel said there are 70 sevens determined upon the nation Israel. The seventieth "week" of Daniel has not yet been fulfilled. The end of the seventieth seven will bring an end or fulfillment to all the visions and prophecies, and the most Holy will be anointed and bring in a kingdom of everlasting righteousness.

Jesus Christ the Messiah was cut off

after 69 sevens without receiving His kingdom. He did not bring in the age of everlasting righteousness, as is so evident today by the world in which we live. The most Holy has not yet been anointed. Therefore, all the prophecies in Daniel have not yet been fulfilled. We have the seventieth seven-year period yet to be completed.

The angel continued to tell Daniel, "The prince [the false messiah or Antichrist] that shall come . . . shall confirm the convenant with many for one week." In the midst of the week, or in the midst of the final seven-year period, he will break the covenant and set up the abomination which causes desolation.[12]

The disciples once asked Jesus what would be the signs of the end of the world. He replied, "When ye therefore shall see the abomination of desolation, spoken of by Daniel the prophet, stand in the holy place, (whoso readeth, let him understand:) then let them which be in Judea flee into the mountains: let him which is on the housetop not come down to take any thing out of his house: neither let him which is in the field return back to take his clothes."[13] The fact that Jesus referred to this event as future in His day precludes any interpretation that would place the seventieth seven in past history.

What is the "abomination of desolation" that Daniel the prophet spoke about? The Antichrist will make a covenant with the nation Israel. He will grant them the right to rebuild their temple in Jerusalem and will promise to bring them peace. Then, after three and one-half years the Antichrist will violate the covenant and will cause the daily sacrifices and oblations in Jerusalem to cease. He'll stand in the holy place of the rebuilt temple and declare that he alone is God. He will demand to be worshiped as God. Then the eyes of the Jews will be opened to see that they have been deceived by this man. That is what is known as the abomination of desolation. From that day it will be only 1,290 days until Jesus comes again in glory.[14]

If anybody claims that Chuck Smith gave the day that Jesus is coming again, they are correct in a sense. Jesus is coming 1,290 days after the Anti-christ creates the abomination of desolation in the temple. When will that day be? We just don't know yet.

Electronic Funds Transfer

The Antichrist will cause everyone to receive a number or a mark in his right hand or forehead. No one will be able to buy or sell without that number. The number will be some form of 666.[15]

Ten or twenty years ago we accustomed ourselves to buying with numbers. Various banks offered services using little plastic cards which held your own coded number. You could go to the store with your card, the cashier would run a stamp across it, and you'd sign your name. The item was yours without any exchange of money.

The day is coming when your money will have absolutely no value in buying or selling. The Antichrist will base his monetary program upon a system that transfers funds with coded identification numbers. All transactions will be processed electronically by computers. Those who are on earth after the rapture of the Church will be assigned a number. They won't be able to buy or sell unless they have that number.

On the front of my new Visa card there is a number. But that number doesn't have all the information. Much more information is actually coded onto the strip of magnetic tape on the back of the card. When the firms set up the new computer relays for which these cards have been designed, they will know how much credit I have, and whatever other information will be placed upon the tape. Most major credit cards already carry that magnetic tape which has been specifically designed for the new computer relays.

Soon every store will set your card in a computer relay at point of sale. Already, there are computerized check-cashing security systems in the major Southern California grocery markets.

One large market chain was losing $20,000 a month in bad checks. To solve the problem, the computer industry invented a relay tied right into the banks. Now the cashier can know whether or not you have the money in the bank before you negotiate your check. You place your supermarket card with your check in the relay and your check is either cleared or rejected. It's an excellent system and is saving the markets considerable amounts of money.

Soon all banks will have computerized accounting systems. Presently, many of the banks in the United States are installing computers. They are able to offer you even broader services than before.

Some banks already offer a service that will pay your monthly light bill, water bill, and gas bill directly through your bank. You never need to see your utility bills again! When your bank receives your utility bills, it automatically transfers your funds. At the end of the month your bank statement shows how much money was taken from your account for each utility company. You never have to write another check or spend the postage to mail it. Electronic funds transfer (EFT) saves you all the trouble!

Currently, the whole economy is outdated and in a mess. EFT is an ideal system because it would eliminate the millions of checks each bank must process annually. All transactions of goods and services would be done by computers. It's a perfect solution to many enormous banking problems.

EFT is also an ideal way of controlling theft. If no man can buy or sell without a number, a thief won't be able to sell his stolen goods unless he can produce a number. But the computer would have all the information for each number, and the thief would soon be apprehended.

Stealing money would be useless because you wouldn't be able to buy or sell with money anyhow. People's accounts will all be safely tucked into the memory chip of the computer, and the computer will keep track of their accounts. Think of all the crime this will eliminate. There'll be no more liquor store holdups or service station robberies. EFT will decrease retail crime tremendously. It's a perfect solution for many of today's business problems.

In Europe the World Banking Association already has an international money transfer system in operation called SWIFT—Society for Worldwide Interbank Financial Telecommunications. The Burroughs Corporation has installed two large computers. One is located in Brussels, and the other, a back-up system, is located in Holland.

The purpose of SWIFT is to transmit international banking messages for all the major banks of the world. Payments are internationally transferred, with the computer automatically changing the pounds to lire, or dollars to francs, or whatever the case may be.

Sixty major banks in the United States went on line with the SWIFT computer in Brussels on September 26, 1977. On October 19, 1977, the system was formally inaugurated when Prince Albert of Belgium pushed the golden button before the gathered dignitaries of the world and announced in his official speech, "I, Albert, Prince of Belgium, declare the SWIFT system officially open."

In America many major companies no longer issue payroll checks, but automatically deposit your wages in the bank. These same banks then automatically pay your bills so that you don't need to handle money. You use a credit card to make most of your purchases.

However, there is one major problem with the credit card system. How can the retailer be certain that the person presenting the card is the same one entitled to use that card?

Most criminals arrested in California carry between five and thirty stolen credit cards. When a thief steals a wallet, he's more interested in the credit cards than the money. With a credit card a thief can immediately buy a load of goods for resale before the card is declared as stolen. Even more, a thief could conceivably steal your card and rob your account!

Technologists are presently working on a foolproof identification system to eliminate the problem of lost or stolen credit cards.

A laser beam has been developed that can painlessly brand livestock in one thirty-two thousandths of a second. The laser beam can also be used for micro-data processing. The entire Bible can now be printed on the head of a pin.

It would be very easy to write your complete personal history on a convenient spot on your body, such as your hand, by laser beam. The information would be invisible to your eyes, because it would be hidden between the cells. But it would all be there.

I don't know whether or not a tattoo by laser beam will be the ultimate answer for identification purposes, but it does present a very good answer. The tattooing would be totally painless and would provide a sure-fire identity that no one could duplicate or steal. Imagine a person walking into a store and setting *your* hand under the scanner to buy *his* goods!

The Bible states that the man who will arise from the federation of European nations will order everyone to receive a mark either on his right hand or his forehead. No one will be able to buy or sell without the mark and the number of the leader's name.

It looks as if we're coming so close to this today. Grocery stores already have cash registers where the checker runs a little electronic scanner over the uniform product code (UPC) on the items that you have selected. Then the special cash register prints out the items and the amounts. As they now run the items under the little scanners, it would also be very simple to hold your hand with its tattooed number under the scanner—and your total grocery bill would be automatically deducted from your computerized bank account!

The capacities for such procedures have already been developed.

Several states presently have small computer relay banks in airports. You just put your bank card in, type out your code, and withdraw your money automatically from the relay station.

The whole world economic system is moving towards electronic funds transfer. EFT computers are already in operation in Europe, and the top banks in the United States are connected to the main computers in Brussels and Holland. The systems are coming together. More and more we see the fantastic bookkeeping capacities of computers and the tremendous advantages that can be gained by using them.

What the Bible predicted about 2,000 years ago was a scientific fantasy at the time, but it has become a practical reality today as we watch the development of computer technology.

The Stage Is Set

According to Biblical prophecy, the nation Israel must be reestablished so that the other end times prophecies can be fulfilled.[16] Israel's rebirth is a vital link in the chain of world events. We need not look to the future for this. Israel was reestablished in 1948.

God has set the stage. The row of dominoes is aligned. Israel is again a nation. The ten European nations are coming together. The electronic funds transfer system is already in progress.

There remains one event to trigger a reaction setting off the final events before Christ returns in glory. The ten-nation confederacy cannot become a world governing power and the Antichrist cannot then step into control until God reckons with the atheistic nation of Russia and the Church is taken out at the rapture. (See *Snatched Away!* by the author for study of rapture.)

Prophetically speaking, it is not clear which imminent event—Russia's invasion of Israel or the rapture of the Church—will occur first. Either event could take place first, with the other immediately following. The Church may or may not see Russia invade Israel. It's not necessary that we do. But it is certain that before the "man of sin" is revealed, the Church will be taken out.

Paul said, "Now we beseech you, brethren, by the coming of our Lord Jesus Christ, and by our gathering together unto him, that ye be not soon shaken in mind, or be troubled, neither by spirit, nor by word, nor by letter as from us, as the day of Christ is at hand."

In other words, Jesus hasn't come yet. Some folks are saying that He has already come and established His Kingdom. Not so! "Let no man deceive you by any means: for that day shall not come, except there come a falling away first."[17]

The term "falling away" is an interesting translation of the Greek word *apostasia*. The root verb from which *apostasia* comes means "to depart from." This verb is used fifteen times in the New Testament, and only once is it translated "fall away." In the other instances it is translated "to depart from" or "to leave from."

Tyndale, one of the first to translate the Bible into English, and many other early translators of the New Testament, translated this Greek word *apostasia* as "a departure." If you read it that way—"For that day shall not come, except there come a departure first, and that man of sin be revealed, the son of perdition"—it could very easily refer to the departure, or rapture, of the Church.

Paul continues, "For the mystery of iniquity doth already work: only he who now letteth [is hindering] will let [will hinder], until he be taken out of the way. And then shall that Wicked [one] be revealed, whom the Lord shall consume with the spirit of his mouth, and shall destroy with the brightness of his coming: Even him, whose coming is after the working of Satan with all power and signs and lying wonders, and with all deceivableness of unrighteousness **in them that perish**; because they received not the love of the truth, that they might be saved."[18]

The Antichrist will be revealed to those who shall perish, because they did not believe the truth that they might be saved. He cannot be revealed until he who hinders is taken out of the way. The hindering force that is keeping the Antichrist from being revealed today is the power of the Holy Spirit working within the Church.

After Jesus Christ takes His Church away, the man of sin will be revealed. He will establish a covenant with Israel and promise to help them in rebuilding their temple.

The last time we visited Israel, the Israelis explained that they do not believe Jesus to be the Messiah because we call Him the Son of God. The Jews do not believe the Messiah will be the Son of God. They believe the Messiah is a man, probably coming out of Europe, who will help them rebuild their temple and bring them peace. The Jewish rabbis are expecting this man to come soon, and the Israelis are ready to hail him as their savior, their Messiah. This is the current religious mental attitude in Israel. The Jews are waiting for Messiah and expecting him almost any time.

The Antichrist will do just as the Jews expect. But after three and one-half years he will stand in the Jerusalem temple and claim to be God. He'll demand to be worshiped as God and he'll cause the daily Jewish oblations and sacrifices to cease.[19]

At this point, the wrath of God such as has never been experienced before will be poured out upon the earth. Then, 1,290 days later Jesus shall return with His Church and with the saints of God, coming in clouds and great glory. He shall establish the Kingdom of God, and His righteousness shall never end.

Preparation

Peter said, "Seeing then that all these things shall be dissolved, what manner of persons ought ye to be?"[20] We're coming down to the wire. What kind of a person ought I to be?

First of all, I should be a spiritual person. God is going to shake this earth until everything that can be shaken will be shaken, until only that which cannot be shaken will remain.[21] If my life is only involved in the material things of this world, then I'm going to experience a total loss when the shaking comes. If my life is totally invested in spiritual things, I won't lose a thing! Thus, I should be spiritually-minded.

But I should also be diligent. I should not quit my job. I should not borrow as much long-term money as I possibly can. The Lord told us to "occupy" until He comes.[22]

As we look at the world scene today, it would appear that the coming of the Lord is very, very close. Yet, we do not know when it will be. It could be that the Lord will wait for a time longer.

If I understand Scripture correctly, Jesus taught us that the generation which sees the "budding of the fig tree," the birth of the nation Israel, will be the generation that sees the Lord's return.[23] I believe that the generation of 1948 is the last generation. Since a generation of judgment is forty years and the Tribulation period lasts seven years, I believe the Lord could come back for His Church any time before the Tribulation starts, which would mean anytime before 1981. (1948+40−7=1981).

However, it is possible that Jesus is dating the beginning of the generation from 1967, when Jerusalem was again under Israeli control for the first time since 587 B.C. We don't know for sure which year actually marks the beginning of the last generation.

Nevertheless, we should live as though the Lord were coming today, because He just might! Be diligent about the things of the Lord and yet practical about your life. Don't quit your job. Don't quit school. But all the while look up and lift up your head, for your redemption is drawing nigh!

Chapter 2

End Times, Part 2

As we studied in Chapter 1, the angel of the Lord told Daniel that seventy sevens are determined upon the nation Israel. Sixty-nine of those sevens have already been fulfilled.

The angel also said that the time span between the commandment to restore and rebuild Jerusalem to the coming of the Messiah will be exactly 483 years.[1] Just as the angel said, Jesus Christ the Messiah was cut off without receiving His kingdom. The Jews were dispersed by the Romans in 70 A.D.

Since the crucifixion of Jesus, God's calendar has stood still. One important seven-year period, the seventieth seven of Daniel which has not been fulfilled, is yet to come. This seventieth seven of Daniel will complete the entire prophecy of Daniel 9. Jesus Christ made the reconciliation for our sins at His first coming. He made an end of our iniquities through His death on the cross. But the latter portion of the prophecy, "to bring in everlasting righteousness . . . and to anoint the most Holy," will be fulfilled at the end of the final seven-year period.

During this last seven-year period the man of sin, or the son of perdition, will be revealed. Jesus Christ referred to him as the one who shall come in his own name and whom the Jews will receive.[2] This man of sin will arise from a confederation of ten European nations.

This man, the Antichrist, will establish a completely new economic system. Money, as such, will be done away with. Financial interactions will be accomplished through electronic funds transfers. Everyone will be assigned a number to be eventually marked upon his body. No one will be able to buy or sell without this number. This system was prophesied in Revelation 13 almost 2,000 years ago, and today we see the development of technology that will make it a reality.

In Brussels there is a giant economic computer, and in Holland there is another computer serving as a back-up system. Many banks in the United States have plugged into this computer already.

Also, according to our government, every person in the United States will soon be assigned a new identification number.[3] Social Security cards are simply too easy to obtain—and many people have several. Aliens are also causing problems with our present identification program. So, a reidentification system has been proposed.

Your new identification number will be your number for life. The government plans to assign a number to each baby the moment he is born. This system will eliminate the problems of identification.

However, as long as the number is on a card, whether it be paper or plastic, the possibility of forgery, theft, or simply borrowing someone else's number exists.

As a woman in the grocery store pulled her credit card out of her purse, she said, "Wouldn't it be nice if they could attach this thing to my body so I wouldn't lose it anymore!" They won't affix the credit card to your body, but they'll have another classification system worked out. No man will be able to buy or sell unless he has this number in his right hand or his forehead.

Today, this checkless-cashless economic system is technically possible. Already international banks are using electronic funds transfers. In fact, I understand that the amount of money presently transferred through the EFT in the United States every week equals the amount of our national debt. It seems unbelievable! But this new economy predicted in the Bible has to come.

Russian Power
In Chapter 1 I pointed out that the Bible predicts a ten-nation European confederacy will rise to power and become the last world-governing empire.

Today, the European Community (EC) consists of nine nations and is currently processing Greece as the tenth nation. If things continue on schedule, Greece will be ratified as a full-fledged member by 1980. This will make the EC a ten-nation European confederation.

But as we look at the world scene today, we recognize one major stumbling block preventing the EC from becoming a world-governing power. And that is Russia. The EC cannot rise to predicted prominence as long as Russia poses such a tremendous threat to the European continent.

Reader's Digest reported that Russia has 20,000 tanks in Eastern Europe ready to move into Western Europe. The Russians have built up tremendous military might while NATO is deteriorating.[4] The ten European nations can never rise to major prominence until the Russian threat is removed. And God has a unique plan to take care of Russia.

How will God handle Russia? How will the ten European nations become a world power? And how will the Antichrist take over as the leader of these ten nations and bring the world under his power? The answer is found in the Book of Ezekiel.

Ezekiel saw a valley of dry bones. God asked Ezekiel, "Can these bones be made to live again?" Ezekiel said, "Lord, you know." Then he watched the valley of dry bones come together—the toe bone connected to the foot bone, the foot bone connected to the ankle bone, and the ankle bone connected to the shin bone. God brought them together and formed a skeleton. Then Ezekiel saw flesh form upon the skeleton, muscles were given to it, and it soon stood upright.

God prophesied to Ezekiel, "So I will make my people to live again though they have been scattered. I will bring them back into the land, and they shall dwell there. I will put my Spirit in them, and I will plant them in the land. I will put flesh upon them, and I will put muscle upon them." God spoke of how He would gloriously resurrect the nation of Israel in the last days.[5]

Then God said, "When I have brought them back into the land, I will put an evil thought into the minds of the leaders of Magog." Magog throughout history has been known as that vast area north of the Caucasus Mountains. Today, it is known as Russia. God continued, "I will bring thee [Russia] out of the north quarters and all of thy bands with thee."

God even listed the nations that would be allied with Russia. And, in most cases, the countries God listed are Russia's allies today! But there will be a few changes. For instance, Iran (presently a friend of Israel) will ultimately side with Russia.

God then said, "I will bring thee [Russia] forth with all your bands against the nation of Israel. I will put hooks into your jaw and I will lead thee forth." God is going to lead Russia into Israel for the slaughter. He declared, "When you have come into the mountains of Israel, my fury shall arise in my face and I will turn thee back." God then describes the destruction that will fall upon this invading Russian army.[6]

In Ezekiel 39 God goes on to give us the details of the destruction. He will leave but a sixth part of the invading Russian army. Five-sixths will be destroyed! The Israelis will be burning the implements of war for seven years. Seven months after the battle is over, professional men will begin burying the bones of the dead soldiers.

It is an interesting point that Israel will not start burying the dead for seven months. It is also interesting that nobody will touch those bones, and professional men will be hired for the purpose of burying the bones. When a person sees a skeleton, he will place a marker by it so the professional buriers can come and bury the bones. It will take seven months to bury the carcasses that have fallen in the land of Israel. Remember this fact. Further on I'll explain the significance of this prophecy in light of Israel's present nuclear potential.

God declared, "When I have brought them again from the people, and gathered them out of their enemies' lands, and am sanctified in them in the sight of many nations; then shall they know that I am the Lord their God . . . Neither will I hide my face any more from them: for I have poured out my spirit upon the house of Israel."[7]

This is a significant moment. When God again pours out His Spirit upon the nation Israel, His great time clock will be started once again, and we'll be at the beginning of the *last* seven-year period.

Russia's invasion of Israel plays a key part in the total plan of God. This invasion will actually trigger the beginning of the end. Once the last seven-year period is finished, Jesus Christ will come again in glory and He will be anointed as King of Kings and Lord of Lords. And so God's everlasting kingdom will be established upon the earth.

It is my very strong conviction that before God's Spirit is placed upon Israel, the Church will be taken out of the earth. The Bible says, "Blindness in part is happened to Israel, until the fulness of the Gentiles be come in."[8] When God no longer nationally blinds Israel but has poured His Spirit upon His people, it precludes the Church from being here.

Today, the Spirit and anointing of God is upon the Church. The Spirit of God has been moving upon the world, drawing out a bride for Jesus Christ. But when that body of believers is completed, when the fullness of the Gentiles has come in, then God's Spirit will again deal with the nation Israel. God will take them back and acknowledge them as His people once again.

Also, this decisive defeat of the Russian army will give the ten European nations the opportunity to rise to immediate power. The confederation of ten nations will then be the unchallenged major power on the European continent.

This, then, is the next major event that we're watching for: Russia's invasion of Israel.

Close Call

I would like to point out how close we came to the end of the Church Age in October, 1973.

At two p.m. October 6, 1973, during Yom Kippur (the most holy day of the year for the Jews), Syria and Egypt simultaneously attacked Israel from opposite ends of the country. The majority of the Israelis and the army personnel were in their synagogues or resting quietly at home. Radios had

46

been silent all day in respect of the Yom Kippur holy day. Suddenly, sirens began to wail in Tel Aviv and Jerusalem. Radios immediately came alive with emergency code numbers for the nation's military troops. The call also went out to the people in the reserve to activate and defend themselves. The Arabs had launched what was intended to be "The War of Annihilation."

The Syrians attacked on the Golan Heights with 1,200 tanks in the initial attack. When Hitler made his major invasion of Russia in World War II he used 1,000 tanks over a 200-mile perimeter. In 1973 Israel was attacked by Syria with 1,200 tanks over a 20-mile perimeter.

In the Sinai, Egypt attacked with 3,000 tanks and 1,000 pieces of major artillery. It was intended to be the War of Annihilation, and it almost was. Were it not for the intervening grace of God, were it not for miracles which were greater than the miracles of the 1967 War, Israel would not be a nation today. Miracles as great as those in Bible days took place when the Syrians and Egyptians attacked Israel with forces far superior in number and oftentimes in weaponry. A miracle of God preserved this little nation.

We still do not fully understand why Syria stopped her attack and hesitated in the Golan Heights. There are many stories of bravery and personal heroism. As Zechariah prophesied, some of the insignificant soldiers became as David.[9]

"Zwicka" is the nickname of Lieutenant Zvi Greengold. He was with his family at Kibbutz Lochamei Hagetaot when the war broke out. He immediately put on his uniform and hitchhiked to the headquarters at Nafech on the Golan Front. He asked for a tank command and was told that three damaged tanks were coming in for repairs and, with another tank that was available, he would head the Zwicka Unit on the Tapline route.

Lieutenant Greengold soon found himself in the thick of battle. He managed to knock out several Syrian tanks but, in the meantime, lost his support tanks. He realized that he would have to leave the main road to survive, and he began maneuvering his tank from behind the knolls.

Zwicka would pop up over a knoll, destroy one of the Syrian tanks, then turn to another knoll and repeat his action. He was knocking out so many Syrian tanks that they thought a whole Israeli brigade was facing them. So, the Syrians retreated!

With odds of 50 to 1 against him, Zwicka turned back the Syrian attack that night. He kept radioing to headquarters that the Zwicka Unit had destroyed another Syrian tank, and headquarters thought Zwicka had a whole tank unit. But he was there all alone holding off the Syrian advance. His is only one of countless stories of David-like heroism to come out of the Yom Kippur War.

The Syrians easily poured through the southern section of the Golan where the defenses had been depleted. The Syrians came within one mile of the Golani headquarters of the Israeli Army. At the time that Syria began her attack, the Israelis only had two tanks and ten men in headquarters at the Golan Heights. Though wave after wave of Syrian tanks moved in, strangely they stopped a mile from army headquarters.

Later, the Golan Heights commander (who is not a godly man at all), laughed and said the Syrians got such a good view of the Sea of Galilee that they stopped to look! He confesses himself that he really doesn't know why they stopped their unrestrained advance.

It is speculated that since the Syrians weren't able to move through the northern sector, they figured that the Israelis had set a trap for them in the south. They may have suspected that the Israelis were letting them pour freely through on the south in order to trap them. That is one theory to explain why the Syrian army halted their advance.

The Syrians didn't know that on the first day of the war they could have marched all the way to Tiberias. They could have taken the whole Galilee region.

Down in the Sinai the Egyptians were planning to take the Bar-Lev line within twenty-four hours. They took it in five hours. They were so surprised with their quick success that they just waited there. They didn't have any contingency plans for moving further so soon. They were not aware that the only obstacles between them and Tel Aviv were ninety battered Israeli tanks. Mysteriously, both Syrians and Egyptians halted long enough to give the Israelis a chance to mobilize and counterattack both in the Golan and in Egypt.

When the Israelis began their counterattack in the Golan Heights, they pushed the Syrians back until Israeli tank forces came within twelve miles of Damascus. Israel then set up a ring around the Syrian capitol, ready to bombard it with the 155 mm. 17-mile range cannons mounted on their tanks. Israel was about to begin an artillery barrage of Damascus.

In the Sinai, General Arik Sharon in a brilliant move crossed the Suez Canal with an assault force and trapped the whole Egyptian Third Army on the Sinai peninsula. The Egyptian Third Army was totally dependent upon the Israelis for their food and medicine.

At this time Soviet Premier Brezhnev

cabled President Nixon and told him that Russia would begin unilateral action to bring peace in the Middle East.

Just hours after the war had started, Russian cargo planes were landing in Egypt and Syria and providing fresh supplies. These planes were on their way to the Mideast before the war ever started. On October 6, 1973, Russian ships landed in Alexandria, Egypt, and in the Syrian port of Latakia with fresh supplies.

Three days before the war started, Russia sent up spy satellites designed to photograph and monitor Israel. The Arab attack was originally scheduled for six p.m. on Yom Kippur, but the satellite showed the Israelis had begun to mobilize. So, the attack was moved ahead by four hours.

Russian soldiers were manning the invading tanks, because Syria didn't have enough trained personnel to command the tanks. In fact, many Russian soldiers driving Syrian tanks were captured by the Israelis on the Golan Heights.

We were in Israel during the '73 War. On our way from Tel Aviv to our hotel in

Bat Yam, we were talking to our cab driver. He was a lieutenant in the army and we were his last fare. As soon as he dropped us off, he had to report for duty. We told him we'd be praying for him because this time it looked as if the war was really a tough one.

He said, "Yes, it is. We're fighting the Russians this time."

I agreed and said, "The Russians have moved in some sophisticated equipment. The SAM-6's are really potent weapons. You're fighting against sophisticated Russian weapons this time."

He said, "I didn't say Russian weapons. We're fighting against the Russians. We've already captured several of them in the Golan Heights."

In a single air battle in the Sinai, five Russian MIGS were shot down. All five were piloted by Russians. Russia had moved a heavy cruiser with nuclear warheads on its decks into Alexandria. This was spotted by U.S. reconnaissance planes.

When Brezhnev notified President Nixon in 1973 that Russia would take unilateral action to bring peace to the

Middle East, he was saying that Russia was preparing to invade Israel. The war had started to turn against Egypt and Syria. In fact, the Russian cargo planes that were bringing supplies to the Arabs were reassigned and were being loaded with Russian paratroopers. Russia was planning to launch a paratroops attack against Israel.

When Russia took over Czechoslovakia during the rebellion in 1968, the first thing Russia did was to send in paratroopers to take over the airport. Once Russian troops captured the airport and sealed it off, they immediately brought in their supplies and tanks and were able to move from the heart of the country to put down the rebellion. It's a new Russian technique of warfare.

Therefore, when Brezhnev cabled the threat to Nixon, our president put the United States troops on alert around the world. Kissinger began fast-paced trips from Israel to Syria to Cairo in an effort to hammer out a peace settlement and a quick cease-fire—before Russia moved in her troops. For a moment World War III was in the balances.

We came close to seeing the end in 1973, but God had other purposes. So, He brought the war to a halt.

Looking back, the Israelis feel that they made a mistake in halting their advances. They were robbed from a true and decisive victory over the Arabs. They could have brought Damascus under the fire of their tanks, forcing the city to surrender.

General Sharon was pleading for permission to move against Cairo while he had the momentum going with him and the Egyptian Army trapped. But he was stopped, and the Jews were kept from a decisive victory. As a result, the Israelis today feel that they're right back where they started.

Syria has now doubled her arsenal of weapons compared to the beginning of the Yom Kippur War. Some sources say that Syria has even tripled her strength.

Over 1,200 Russian advisors are instructing the Iraqis how to use 1,000 tanks and 300 planes which Russia has supplied. This includes the newest Russian long-range bomber which no other nation in the world except Russia possesses. Israel is now easily within range of these bombers.

Russia is giving tremendous military support to Syria, Iraq, and the Arab states.

Also, Egypt has been gearing up for war again. Israel charges that the Egyptian troops are violating the Sinai Agreement. According to the agreement, the Egyptians were not to have over 8,000 troops along the Suez. They've recently moved in 18,000 to 20,000 troops. The Israelis say that this is a definite violation and a threat to their security.

Recently, Syrian President Assad declared that the peace talks have fallen apart. It's ridiculous to go to Geneva. And the only solution is to go into Israel by force, take the West Bank, and give it to the Palestinians.

Israeli Attitude Changing

It is very interesting to notice the Israelis' change of attitude since the 1973 War. The Israelis used to have "the Masada complex." That is, suicide is preferable to slavery.

When the Roman General Silvaenus

was making his final assault against the elevated city of Masada in 72 A.D., the 960 inhabitants saw that the Romans had built a tremendous ramp towards the rear of their fortress. They knew that in the morning the Romans would enter the city and they would not be able to hold off the Romans' assault. Ben El'azar called the people together in the synagogue and announced that they would either see their children led off to slavery and their wives ravaged before their eyes, or they could take the honorable way and commit mass suicide. The people decided on suicide rather than slavery.

Each man gathered together with his family. Ten men were chosen to go through the city of Masada and systematically kill the children, then the wife, and then the husband in each family. The husband and wife kissed their children goodbye, and the husband kissed his wife. They then laid down on the floor and their throats were slit.

The ten remaining men gathered together in a room. They drew coins numbered one through ten to choose who would be the last to die. As nine men lay on the floor, the man chosen to die last slit their throats. After he made sure they were dead, he then committed suicide.

The next morning the Romans broke into the city of Masada. To their horror they discovered that the city's inhabitants, with the exception of one old lady and a few young children who had hidden in a cave, were all dead. It was an empty victory for Rome.

Even to this day, when the Jewish cadets graduate, they are taken to Masada for their graduation exercises. The leaders recount the story of Masada and then the whole group declares together: "Masada shall not fall again!" In other words, they too feel that suicide is preferable to slavery. They'll fight until they die.

However, the Masada complex is being replaced in Israel by a new attitude called "the Samson complex." Samson also committed suicide but, when he did, he took his enemies with him. When he knew it was the end, Samson had a little boy lead him to the pillars that were the main supports of the building. When he reached the pillars, Samson bowed with all his strength and pulled the pillars in so that 3,000 Philistines were crushed along with him.[10]

Today, the Israelis say that if they have to go, they'll take the world with them. They feel—and for good reason—that the world has let them down.

In the Yom Kippur War, after ten days of fighting, the Israelis almost ran out of ammunition. The United States could not help them because Germany, England, Italy, and France would not let us land and refuel our supply planes on their soil. Finally, after ten days, Portugal opened up a base on the Azores for refueling. Our planes were soon landing almost nose to tail at the Tel Aviv airport, resupplying the Israeli army just in time to keep them ahead in the war.

Israel feels that Europe has let her down. She says, "If we fall, why should we care if the world also falls?"

General Arik Sharon, who led the brilliant counterattack across the Suez Canal trapping the Third Egyptian

Army, was talking to one of the U.S. senators visiting Israel. General Sharon said that if another war erupts in the Mideast, the U.S. won't have to worry about an Arab oil embargo. He pointed out that Entebbe (where Israelis completed a successful commando attack) is 2,000 miles from Tel Aviv . . .but Tripoli is only 900 miles away. General Sharon said that his men will "take care" of the oil situation in case there's another war.

The Israelis are planning to go all out in the next war. They have declared that they will not stop until every arm lifted against them has been destroyed. They intend to take over or destroy the Saudi Arabian oil fields. Saudi Arabia has been allocating one billion dollars annually to the Arab states for the next conflict. The Israelis feel Saudi Arabia should not go unpunished. It is Israel's full intention to go all out the next time with everything she's got.

What will this do? When Israel begins to exercise the advantage in the next conflict and starts sending paratroopers to Saudi Arabia to take over the oil fields, you can be sure that Russia will try to stop Israel by force.

As soon as Russia moves against Israel, the final countdown will begin. We'll then be at the scene that God had described in Ezekiel 38 and 39. Russia's invasion of Israel is the first event that will trigger the sequence of events during the final seven years: the emergence of the ten-nation power, the rise of the Antichrist, the Great Tribulation during the last half of the seven years, and then the glorious coming of Jesus Christ with His Church in power and glory! And finally, the establishment of His Kingdom bringing in everlasting righteousness.

Where does that place the Church? When God's Spirit is again poured upon the nation Israel or Russia is decisively defeated, the door will be open for the emergence of the Antichrist—which places the Church out of here!

Paul said, "Behold, I show you a mystery; we shall not all sleep, but we shall all be changed, in a moment, in the twinkling of an eye."[11] We do not know exactly when the Church will be caught up in relation to Russia's attack on Israel. The Church could be taken out before Russia ever invades Israel or during the time of the battle. We shall certainly be taken out by the time God destroys Russia and again puts His Spirit on the nation Israel.

War clouds are hanging over Israel right now. Syria has fully armed herself and her president is threatening to forcibly recapture the West Bank—and Israel refuses to give it back. The whole Mideast situation could explode again at any moment. Most of the Israelis with whom I've talked are anticipating conflict at any time.

That excites me because if war breaks out—and it's certainly within the realm of probability—very soon we could be rejoicing around the throne of God in glory! Keep your eye on the Middle East. Things are getting more serious there every day.

Israel's Nuclear Potentials

The Israelis have indicated that they now possess nuclear weapons. In fact, during the very crucial moment early in the 1973 War when it looked as if Israel would be defeated, Israel may have been activating some of her nuclear bombs. Israel has often declared that she can't afford to lose.

In 1977 there were indications that Israel possessed a neutron bomb—a weapon the United States was still developing in the same year. The neutron bomb is that great "humanitarian bomb" that only kills people but doesn't destroy buildings or other weapons. It is designed to kill by ultra-high radiation.

In his book *Hiroshima*, John Hersey describes the effects of the atomic bomb dropped on Hiroshima. Many people who were not killed by the initial blast died from the ultra-high radiation. He describes how eyeballs melted and poured down people's faces.[12] Sores that would not heal broke out upon their bodies, and their flesh consumed away as a result of exposure to the high radiation.

The effects of radiation from the bomb exploded in Hiroshima are very similar to those the neutron bomb is designed to cause. It's horrifying.

That is why I find Ezekiel 39 so interesting. God specifically points out the fact that the people don't touch the bones of the victims for seven months. Finally, professional buriers are used to bury the carcasses. Nobody else wants to touch the bones for fear of contamination. Ezekiel perfectly describes the results of death by radioactivity.

The Lord told Zechariah that His people would come back into the land of Israel and Jerusalem would be inhabited again. Jerusalem shall become "a burdensome stone" to all of her neighbors round about. Whoever seeks to come against Jerusalem will be destroyed, though the whole world be gathered together against her—which seems to be happening today! The Lord will defend the inhabitants of Jerusalem and the least of them "shall be as David."[13]

Then the Lord said, "This shall be the plague wherewith the Lord will smite all the people that have fought against Jerusalem; their flesh shall consume away while they stand upon their feet, and their eyes shall consume away in their holes, and their tongue shall consume away in their mouth."[14] Twenty-five hundred years ago God described the effects of the super-radiation of a neutron bomb! I can't say that's exactly how Israel will defeat Russia, but certainly the description in Zechariah is very interesting to study.

We are living in the *last* of the last days. At any moment the Middle East can erupt into a conflict that will be the war of annihilation this time of the Arabs by the Israelis. Israel will be going all out, which will undoubtedly prompt Russia's involvement. Then the Lord will take us, the Body of Christ, out of the whole mad scene and into the heavenly glories of God.

Jesus said, "When these things begin to come to pass, then look up, and lift up your heads; for your redemption draweth nigh."[15]

It is later than you think. It is time you woke up from your lethargy and realize that the coming of the Lord is at hand! If you've been playing around with Christianity and playing around with your relationship with God, it's high time to realize you need a full-on commitment to Jesus Christ. There's no time to waste. The Bridegroom is coming. He's even at the door waiting.

Make sure you'll be ready when He comes.

If you wait till you read the headlines, "Arab States Attack Israel," you may have waited too long, because the Church may not even be here to see the invasion. I would encourage you now, while you yet can, to dedicate your life to Jesus Christ. Submit yourself to Him—and you too will rejoice when you see the appearing of our great God and Saviour, Jesus Christ.

Chapter 3

Warning

Normally, when we think of the end of the world, we immediately picture an old gray-bearded man carrying a sandwich board. One side of the board says "Repent" and the other side says "The End of the World is Near." He walks with starry eyes in the midst of the crowd crying, "Repent!"

But I'm hearing a lot of talk today about the end of the world, not from old men with sandwich boards, but from college professors and leading scientists.

Signs of the Times

Recently, there's been a great deal of concern about the ozone blanket around the earth.¹ Ozone is a form of oxygen. Oxygen has two atoms to the molecule, and ozone has three atoms to the molecule. The third atom is held by the other two atoms. Ozone is a very unstable gas. The third atom easily escapes and easily combines with others, which makes ozone such an excellent cleaning compound.

The earth is surrounded with a blanket of ozone gas in the stratosphere. This ozone gas plays a very important part in our survival on planet earth. It acts as a filter and protects us from bombardment of the sun's lethal ultraviolet rays.

In the Book of Job God mentions a "swaddlingband" around the earth.² God may have been referring to the ozone layer that surrounds the earth. If the ozone layer were brought down to the earth's surface, it would form a blanket only three feet thick.

Our scientists are now saying that we're in danger of destroying this protective ozone layer. Aerosol products release gases into the air which cause the ozone to combine with nitrogen gas and form nitric oxide. Unless we do something, such as change the gas within the aerosol cans, we will continue to eradicate the ozone blanket.

The new supersonic jets that fly 1500 miles an hour at 55,000 feet are also a grave threat to the ozone blanket. The gases emitted through the exhausts of these supersonic jets are also combining with the ozone blanket, diminishing the blanket's ability to protect the earth.

In addition, the testing of atomic bombs releases great clouds of gases into the atmosphere which are detrimental to the existing ozone blanket. If we were to have an atomic war, with a number of atomic devices let loose within the atmosphere, the worst effect of the atomic bomb wouldn't necessarily be the initial destruction. It could very well be the destruction of the ozone layer. Without this blanket the ultraviolet rays of the sun would begin to cook men alive.

In Revelation 16 we read that, when the fourth vial is poured out by the angel during the Great Tribulation, power is given unto the sun to scorch men with fire.[3] This could very well be a description of the ultraviolet rays penetrating the disappearing ozone blanket and burning those exposed to the sun. This calamity was predicted 2,000 years ago, before anyone even knew that ozone gas existed!

Scientists estimate that unless we take immediate and radical steps to reverse the deterioration of the ozone blanket, we could destroy it within ten years—and the ultraviolet rays of the sun would scorch men upon the earth.

Scientists are saying, "Reverse direction—or it's the end of the world!" That's not much different from the old man with the sandwich board who says, "Repent. It's the end of the world!"

Man is also guilty of recklessly using insecticides. The only way the world can produce enough crops to keep us all from starving to death is by using massive amounts of insecticides. But we don't fully know the consequences and side-effects of these insecticides on our health, lives, or future.

One of the most prominent insecticides is DDT. It has been banned in the United States but not in the other parts of the world.

We have discovered that DDT doesn't disintegrate in the soil but remains in its same chemical form. When it rains, DDT flows into the streams. From the streams this insecticide flows into the rivers and then into the oceans. We are now beginning to discover the tremendous effect DDT has in the ocean. It destroys the seaweed, the plant life, and the fish. Many thriving fishing businesses on the California coast have had to close down as a result of DDT contamination.

It's estimated that perhaps only one-tenth of the DDT used has reached the oceans as yet. We don't know what will happen when the other nine-tenths gets there.

The fact that we may destroy a major portion of the life within the ocean also coincides with another plague spoken of in the Book of Revelation. John saw a great mountain burning with fire fall into the sea, and the third part of the creatures living within the sea were destroyed.[4]

We're also being warned about over-population. Experts predict that unless something dramatic is done to curb the growing population, by the year 2000 the earth will be wall to wall with people. The earth's population has already risen to over four billion people, and it's growing at the rate of 2% of the total population each year. From 1976 to 1977 our population grew by 86 million people![5] Even now we cannot feed all the people on the earth. The majority today goes to bed hungry and undernourished. As the population increases, the demand for food increases, but the supply of food decreases. And so we see food prices rising sky-high.

Jesus said that famines would be one of the signs of the end of the world.[6] Revelation tells of a time that is coming when a "measure of wheat" (or a quart of wheat) will be sold for a day's wage—approximately thirty dollars.[7]

If you want to hedge yourself for the coming catastrophe, don't invest your money in silver or gold. Put it in wheat. What good will your gold be if you can't buy anything with it? In fact, James warns in the last days, "Go to now, ye rich men, weep and howl for your miseries that shall come upon you . . . Your gold and silver is cankered."[8]

Man has also created many destructive weapons. It is estimated that the arsenal of the United States now amounts to the equivalent of 15 tons of TNT for every person alive on the earth.

In talking of the end of the world, Jesus said, "Except those days should be shortened, there should no flesh be saved."[9] For centuries that prophecy of Christ seemed ridiculous. Formerly, if you were to suggest that man could completely self-destruct from the face of the earth, you would've been laughed off stage. People would have thought you were out of your head.

But now we have enough explosive power to destroy every man, woman, and child living on the planet. Our military men are warning us that a major nuclear war could mean the end of the world.

Also, our energy sources are rapidly being depleted. We used to take oil out of the ground as if there were no tomorrow. We thought we certainly had enough energy reserved to last indefinitely. Now we are constantly being asked to curb our normal use of energy, until science can hopefully discover some additional energy sources. Our fossil-fuel energies are limited, and scientists predict the approaching end for fossil-fuel energy.

Scientists are also predicting some very dire earthquakes in 1982 during a rare alignment of the planets. All nine planets within our solar system will be "in line on the same side of the Sun." This rare alignment occurs once every 179 years or so. It will have a tremendous effect upon the gravitational forces of the earth. Scientists predict that tremendous earthquakes will shake our planet in 1982.[10]

Earthquakes are increasing in frequency and intensity around the earth—another sign that Jesus said would signal the end of the world.[11]

The physicists are also getting into the act. In studying the earth's structure, they find that the ions affected by the earth's magnetism are lined up differently from what is now the true North Pole. They predict that the world will soon experience a polar axis flip.

These flips occur approximately every 5,000 years. It's believed that the last polar axis flip coincided with the flood of Noah's time—and this means we're overdue for the next shift! During a polar axis flip islands disappear, mountains turn into valleys, and ocean floors become land masses.

The area of Salt Lake City used to be a vast ocean. There are fossils at 7,000 feet above sea level on the south rim of the Grand Canyon, indicating a major change in the oceans and the mountain structures of the past. Such changes supposedly happened during the last polar axis flip. It is impossible to calculate the geophysical damage that will result from such an upheaval of nature.

Cheer up! If everything else fails, the sun is burning up at the rate of four million tons per second. Giving off such a vast amount of energy allows us to survive here on planet earth, but the sun will only be able to support life for another five billion years. If nothing else gets us, that will in time!

Creation and Termination

It used to be considered scientifically naive to talk about the day of creation, but scientists are now realizing that there must have been such a day. Sir James said that the universe is like a giant clock that was wound up and is slowly running down. With the sun burning off such a tremendous amount of mass every second, had the universe existed from infinity then the sun would have at one time filled all of space. Calculate how much mass has been released from the sun in the past one million years, and add that to the present size of the sun. Then go back ten million years, calculate the mass released, and add that mass to the present size of the sun. If you go back far enough, the sun at one time must have filled the whole universe—and we know that didn't happen. Therefore, it's much more feasible scientifically to talk about the day of creation.

Now scientists are also talking about the day of termination.

Our social scientists are also concerned, but not so much about the physical aspects of the planet as about the men who are living upon the planet. Such scientists are questioning our possibility of surviving even if none of these physical catastrophes take place.

These scientists are alarmed at the rising increase in crime. The police departments and law enforcement agencies are confessing their inability to cope with the sheer number of crimes they have to handle.

Have you called a policeman lately? The police come out and make a report, but they give you very little encouragement about recovering anything stolen or missing. If your child has run away, they file a missing person's report. But there's very little promise of ever finding and bringing him back. So much crime exists that many experts have actually given up any hope of establishing law and order.

Paul wrote to Timothy, "In the last days perilous times shall come. For men shall be . . . without natural affection, truce breakers . . . incontinent, fierce . . . lovers of pleasures more than lovers of God."[12] The Bible describes men as we see them today.

With the scientists, the professors,

the militarists, and the sociologists all crying "The end of the world!"—it seems strange to me that the Church has been so silent. It may be that the Church is so preoccupied with its dwindling role and increased financial burdens that it hasn't noticed the signs of the times.

Perhaps another cause is that people in the past have foolishly and unscripturally set dates for Jesus' return. Even though Jesus said that no man knows the day or the hour,[13] many have come and gone, proclaiming a special revelation of the day and the hour. Perhaps because of this situation the Church has shunned the field of prophecy.

When the disciples said to Jesus, "What will be the sign of the end of the world?" Jesus didn't say, "It's none of your business." Jesus spent two whole chapters telling them the signs preceding the end of the world.[14]

When Daniel cried out, "Lord, how long till the end?" the Lord told him *to the day* when the end would take place.[15]

Real New World

When we, as Christians, talk about

the end of the world, we talk about something entirely different than do the scientists. The scientists are talking about the end of the world in a *physical* sense. But Christians talk about the end of the world based on the Greek word *kosmos*, which means "the set order." The world that is governed by Satan and in rebellion against God is coming to a final and conclusive end.

Man has tried just about every form of government that can be conceived in the human mind—city kingdoms, monarchy, democracy, communism. Man has attempted many different ways to govern himself, but every form of government has ultimately disintegrated. Man cannot govern himself without greed and corruption setting in. Most forms of government have only been able to endure for about 200 years before totally deteriorating.

We, the Church, look for a new form of government: a monarchy that will embrace the entire world. We're waiting for our King to come and set up His monarchy. We're waiting for the Kingdom of God to cover the earth as the waters do cover the sea.

We do not know the day or the hour, but Jesus said, "Watch therefore . . . be ye also ready: for in such an hour as ye think not the Son of man cometh."[16] Then Jesus gave parables by which He illustrated the importance of *watching* and being *ready* for the Lord to come and to receive His Church unto Himself.

The Church has great cause to cry "The end of the world!"—so many signs of the end have already been fulfilled. God has established his nation Israel back in the land as He promised the prophets. Ezekiel tells us that Israel shall no longer be two nations (which was the case when it divided into northern and southern kingdoms in the tenth century B.C.). But Israel will become one nation upon the land, and one king shall rule over them.[17] God also said that Israel shall build again the waste places and they that come from Jacob "shall blossom and bud, and fill the face of the world with fruit."[18]

Israel is now the third largest exporter of fruit in the world. That's amazing when you realize that Israel is smaller than the state of California. Israel is also the main supplier of flowers throughout all of Europe. Because of her good climate and favorable growing conditions, flower growing has become one of Israel's major industries.

God has fulfilled his promise to bring Israel back together and to cause the Israelis to prosper in the land. But also, even as Zechariah said, it seems that now they're almost standing alone against all the nations of the earth. God has promised that He would stand beside them, even though all the nations of the earth be gathered together against them.[19]

The author stated in the Psalms, "When the Lord shall build up Zion, he shall appear in his glory."[20] Christ first came to earth to be crucified. He came humbly. "Behold, thy King cometh unto thee meek, and sitting upon an ass and a colt the foal of an ass."[21] But Jesus is coming the second time with great power and glory! The Psalmist was referring to Christ's second coming— when the Lord shall build up Zion then shall He also appear in His glory. The Church ought to be crying, "The end of the world!" because God has now built up Zion, the land of Israel.

We see in the world today the predicted famines, earthquakes, and pestilences. Doctors are always warning us of new flu strains that are worse than those we've had so far. The flu and viruses are becoming more and more immune to the antibiotics.

The Bible speaks about the "distress of nations, with perplexity."[22] As we look at the nations today, not one strong ruler is governing in the world. Our government has lost credibility and is held in disrespect. The world is divided and the nations are in perplexity. Even the experts don't know what to do about the economic situation, the energy crisis, or the food shortages. There are perplexities of nations just as the Scripture said would take place in the end times.

Men are looking for a leader. A leader is coming and they'll be drawn after him. He's going to come in his own name, proclaiming marvelous things. He's going to have a beautiful economic program by computerizing buying and selling and giving everybody a number. It used to seem far-fetched a few years ago, but it doesn't seem so far-fetched anymore.

Is it all just a coincidence? Or did God know what He was talking about when He spoke of these things 2,000 years ago?

Jesus said, "When these things begin to come to pass, then look up, and lift up your heads; for your redemption draweth nigh."[23] The Church ought to be looking up, expecting and looking for our Lord. We should be proclaiming to the world: "The end of the world!"

Then, as soon as man's present system is destroyed, there will be the beginning of a new world governed by the righteous Son of God. This new world will be filled with peace and love. It will not know war, sickness, suffering, sorrows, pain or death.[24] Jesus shall reign as King of Kings and Lord of Lords. Ours is not a gloomy prediction of the end of the world as is the scientists'. Ours is the glorious prediction of the end of this old world order of man and the beginning of the new world order of Jesus Christ and His love!

Chapter 4

Escape

Our world is in a death-dive. We have peaked-out and now we're plunging rapidly to the end. Moral rottenness and decay have so corrupted our society that we're on a greased skid downward.

The only escape will be when Jesus Christ snatches His followers out of this mad plunge.

Then the rest of the populace will have seven years before the end of the world. The first 3½ years will be a period of "good times." But during the second 3½ years God's wrath will be poured out upon this earth. Jesus described this judgment to come as a time of tribulation such as the world has never seen or will ever see again.[1]

So, how do you become a follower of Jesus Christ and escape the impending destruction?

Main Message

God's main message to us is "Repent." If we *repent* then God will forgive us our sins.

But what does it mean to repent? It doesn't mean just to be sorry, because you can be sorry for the things you've done and, yet, go right on doing them.

"Repent" means to turn away from, to turn your back on, and to forsake. God doesn't want you just to be sorry for your sins. He wants you to be so sorry that you turn from them and quit doing them altogether.

Horror

In the Book of Revelation God gives us a detailed account of the horrors, destruction, and desolation which will come upon our planet earth.

One such horror is that Satan will unlock the abyss in the earth's core and for five months hordes of demonic creatures will roam the earth with the power to inflict torment like that of scorpions. It will be a time of such terrible torment that people will want to kill themselves but, according to the Bible, they won't be able to die. They'll be in a living hell.[2]

Then, after this five-month period, an invading army of 200 million soldiers will wipe out one-third of the earth's population.[3] We think of the outcry over the deaths in the Vietnam war, and rightfully so. But imagine the effects when *one out of three* are massacred by this invading army!

Why?

Why will there be such awful judgment upon the earth so soon? Why such horrible tribulation?

Because people have been guilty of forsaking the laws of God and the way of God. Sin has its own inevitable consequence — death.

God has given us the way to a meaningful and prosperous life. God says, "If you'll follow Me, you'll be happy and peaceful." But man has rejected God and gone after his own way. God describes for us the conditions in the world that will bring judgment.

The Bible says that the people left on the earth in the last days "repented not of the works of their hands, that they should not worship devils, and idols . . . neither repented they of their murders . . . sorceries . . . fornication, nor of their thefts."[4]

First of all, people will be worshiping devils. God wants you to seek His guidance and His wisdom. God wants to guide your life and to give you wisdom about what you should do. But today people are not seeking the guidance or the counsel of God. Instead, they are going to devils for counsel and for guidance. They seek the advice of mediums, psychics, fortune tellers, ouija boards, horoscopes. They are worshiping devils rather than God.

Not only will they worship devils, but they will also worship idols. Everyone bows his knee to some object of worship—some ideal, some principle, some goal, some ambition, or some thing. Every man must worship. This is innate to man. If he doesn't worship

God, then he must and will find a sub-
stitute.

Many Christian college students are
ridiculed by their secular professors
because of their belief in Jesus Christ.
Professors make Christians one of
their favorite targets, mocking and
laughing at those who believe in God.
But then the professor goes home and
worships an idol in his backyard!
Maybe it's his boat, sports car, or a
garden he's cultivating. But every man
has his idol.

Men in the last days will not repent
of their murders and sorceries. The
word "sorceries" in the original Greek
is *pharmakia*, which means "the use of
drugs for thrill or enchantment."

Neither did they repent of their fornication. As we look around the world
today we see the lowering and eradica-
tion of the standards of morality. It
seems that almost every medium of
communication is seeking to destroy
any moral principles that a person or
society possesses.

One young lady who was about to
get married went to a minister for
counseling. The minister asked her,

"Have you been living with your fiance?"

She said, "Of course not!"

He replied, "How do you know whether or not you want to marry him? You should live with him for a few months." Then he charged her $25 for his advice! He wears a robe that distinguishes him as a minister. He's a minister alright, but not of Jesus Christ or of God.

The Lord said that final impending judgment is coming for a variety of reasons. One is the condition of open fornication. It is difficult in this day and age, with the pressures that are being placed upon you, to keep yourself pure. But the Word of God says that you must flee the ungodly lusts that damn men's souls.[5] God's laws have not changed. God's rules have not been altered. They're still the same today.

A young man was working on his doctorate in the science department of a famous university. He said that practically every bit of equipment in the science lab was stolen property. When he refused to do his project on stolen equipment, his fellow students laughed at him. They said he'd never complete his doctorate unless he was willing to steal some kind of equipment to perform his experiments.

We've come to a place where we justify thievery. Today, it's very common to steal on the job. "They're not paying me enough, anyhow! I'll supplement my income." For these things comes the wrath of God upon the earth.

In spite of the invasion of demon hordes and the fact that one-third of the people are massacred, the two-thirds that remain do not repent of their sins. It makes one wonder just what will bring a man to repentance, turn him from his sins and back to God.

Rarely do judgments bring a person to repentance. As a general rule, judgment only hardens an individual's heart against God.

It is the goodness of God that brings a man to repentance.[6] Though you have been guilty of worshiping devils, guilty of having idols, guilty of murder, drugs, fornication, or thievery, God loves you. He loves you so much that He sent His only begotten Son to take the responsibility of the guilt for every wrong you have ever done. Jesus Christ died on the cross in your place so that He could wash you clean from guilt forever.

But you may say, "I'll wait until I see God's judgments come upon this earth, *then* I'll turn to God for mercy." But, if you don't repent now that you hear of the goodness and mercy of God, why would you repent during the time of God's judgments? If the goodness of God doesn't bring you into His family, judgments won't either.

Repentance must be the work of God within your life. No one can bring you to repentance. Someone might bring you to sorrow. I might make you feel very sorry, but I can't make you repent.

You cannot create repentance within yourself. You must allow God to speak to you and touch your heart. Only godly sorrow leads to repentance.

Stop and reflect. Whatever you may be getting out of your experiences of worshiping devils or idols, commiting fornication, or taking drugs, is it worth the sacrifice of your soul? Why not turn your life over to Jesus Christ to-day? He has a much better plan for you!

Footnotes

Introduction & Chapter 1
1. Matthew 24:36 2. 1 Thessalonians 5:1-2, 4
3. Daniel 2 4. Daniel 3:1-7 5. Daniel 4:31-37 6. Daniel
7 7. Revelation 13 8. Zechariah 11:15-17 9. Daniel
9:21-24 10. Daniel 9:25-26 11. Matthew 21:1-11
12. Daniel 9:26-27 13. Matthew 24:15-18 14. Daniel
12:11 15. Revelation 13:16-18 16. Ezekiel 37
17. 2 Thessalonians 2:1-3 18. 2 Thessalonians 2:7-10
19. 2 Thessalonians 2:4; Daniel 9:27 20. 2 Peter 3:11
21. Hebrews 12:26-27 22. Luke 19:13 23. Matthew
24:32-34

Chapter 2
1. Daniel 9:24-25 2. John 5:43 3. "'Let's See Your
I.D.'," *Herald Examiner*, 22 January 1977, p. 1. 4. Sen.
Sam Nunn, "The New Soviet Threat to NATO," *Reader's
Digest*, July 1977, pp. 73-77. 5. Ezekiel 37 6. Ezekiel 38
7. Ezekiel 39:27-29 8. Romans 11:25 9. Zechariah
12:8 10. Judges 16:26-30 11. 1 Corinthians
15:51-52 12. John R. Hersey, *Hiroshima* (New York:
Random House, Inc., 1946), p. 68. 13. Zechariah
12:2-9 14. Zechariah 14:12 15. Luke 21:28

Chapter 3
1. "The Doomsday Effect," *Newsweek*, September 16,
1974, p. 57. 2. Job 38:9 3. Revelation 16:8
4. Revelation 8:8-9 5. "Population," *World Book
Encyclopedia*, 1977, XV, p. 597. 6. Matthew 24:7
7. Revelation 6:6 8. James 5:1-3 9. Matthew 24:22
10. John Gribbin and Stephen Plagemann, *The Jupiter
Effect* (New York: Walker and Company, 1974), pp.
101-105. 11. Matthew 24:7 12. 2 Timothy 3:1-4
13. Matthew 24:36 14. Matthew 24-25 15. Daniel
12:11 16. Matthew 24:42, 44 17. Ezekiel 37:21-22
18. Isaiah 27:6 19. Zechariah 12:3 20. Psalms
102:16 21. Matthew 21:5 22. Luke 21:25 23. Luke
21:28 24. Revelation 21:4

Chapter 4
1. Matthew 24:21 2. Revelation 9:1-6 3. Revelation
9:15-16 4. Revelation 9:20-21 5. 2 Timothy 2:22
6. Romans 2:4

Titles from
MARANATHA!

Available through your bookseller. Write for complete catalog.
Maranatha House Publishers
P.O. Box 1498, Costa Mesa, CA 92626